Name: ___Amina___

Class: ___Super seeker.___

Teacher: _____

Islamic Studies
Textbook Level 2

Minhaj-ul-Quran International

Published by

Minhaj-ul-Quran Publications
30 Brindley Road
Manchester
M16 9HQ (UK)

Acknowledgements

Bilal Hussain, Safina Nazir, Muhammad Zeeshan Qadri, Ali Akbar, Raffiq Patel and M. Dawood Mehmood

A sincere thank you to Ajmal Khan for his assistance in the design work

ISBN: 978-1-908229-56-4

www.minhajpublications.com

www.islamforkids.org.uk

First published August 2018

Printed by Mega Printing in Turkey

proudly sponsored by
letsREVIVE
a project of Minhaj Welfare Foundation
minhajwelfare.org
Registered in England & Wales 1064057 Scotland SC043566

Islamic Studies
Textbook Level 2

Series Editors

Waqas Ahmed Amin

Jawed Iqbal Tahiri

Mariam Khalid

Series Director

Tahseen Khalid

Minhaj-ul-Quran International

Preface

In the name of Allah, the Most Merciful, the Most Kind.

WE PRAISE ALLAH that the Muslim community has come a long way since the days when the first immigrants settled in Britain. From that time till today, there have been significant developments in the quality of educational material being produced by British Muslims. Many advancements have been made in this regard such that English is fast becoming one of the academic languages of Islam, alongside Arabic, Persian, Urdu and Turkish.

The importance of education cannot be overstated. The British Muslim community has put great effort into imparting Islamic knowledge to their children. Islamic classes and religious seminaries have been established up and down the country for the single goal of teaching the coming generations the fundamentals of their religion. Among those that have been at the forefront in this regard is Minhaj-ul-Quran International, a global organisation with branches in over 90 countries.

As an organisation, Minhaj-ul-Quran International seeks to uplift Muslims worldwide through the revival of education and spirituality. It established its first branch in the United Kingdom in the late 1980s and founded its first centre in the 1990s. For more than two decades it has endeavoured to provide for the educational and spiritual needs of the Muslim diaspora of Great Britain.

The 'Islam for Kids' initiative is part of the longstanding services of Minhaj-ul-Quran International. This Islamic Studies series was produced and developed by second and third generation British scholars, who are trained classically in the traditional Islamic sciences, alongside QTS (Qualified Teaching Status) accredited teachers. It is an indigenous and local endeavour by the UK branch of Minhaj-ul-Quran International to fulfil the educational needs of native English-speaking students.

The Syllabus

The 'Islam for Kids' Islamic Studies series has been split into six levels with each level corresponding to the years of the state-funded education system in the UK. It is recommended to start level one at the age of 5 when the child starts year one at primary school and to complete level 6 by the age of 11 when the child completes his or her primary school education. However, the series can be started earlier at an earlier age or later depending on the ability of the student.

The six levels have been grouped into three stages, with each stage consisting of two levels. In the first stage, which consists of levels one and two, the aim is to ease the child into understanding Islamic concepts and terminology. The purpose of this stage is not to burden the child with technical knowledge about Islam, but rather to simply instil in them a sense of Muslim identity and to explore key Islamic concepts.

Traditionally, Muslim parents have been advised to have a play-based approach with their children's learning for the first seven years and then to formally teach them for the next seven years. Following this advice, in the first two years of the syllabus, a more visual approach has been adopted with the text being kept at a minimum. This enables the content to be taught in a child-friendly manner and allows teachers and parents to make the lessons more interactive and engaging for the child.

The second stage of the syllabus begins at level three when the child reaches seven years of age. From this level onwards, a more formal approach to learning is adopted. Many of the concepts in the first stage are revisited, but instead of being largely pictorial, they are more text-based so that the key concepts can be conveyed in detail to the child and to encourage the child to start thinking about the content in more depth.

In the third stage of the syllabus, which consists of levels five and six, the series shifts to a more text-heavy approach. This is to encourage the child to learn independently and practice their key reading and comprehension skills. The content at this level increases in difficulty to engage students academically and to raise the standard of literacy and understanding of Islamic concepts.

The concepts from the previous two stages are revisited in this third stage but in much more detail. Parents and teachers alike will find this stage beneficial as reading material to help prepare in terms of subject knowledge for teaching the lessons in the earlier two stages. In this way, the three stages work together to ease the child into becoming well acquainted with Islamic terminology, concepts and values.

By the end of this syllabus, the child will have acquired the essential Islamic knowledge (*Fard `Ayn*) for them to be able to live their life as a practising Muslim. This Islamic Studies series is an excellent resource for parents to lay the foundation for their child's learning. If Allah wills, further levels will be added to this syllabus, thus enhancing the child's understanding of Islam and enabling them to become lifelong learners of the Islamic tradition.

The First Edition

In preparation of this series, authentic and reliable content was taken from the works of great scholars who represent Islamic orthodoxy. Some of the books that were consulted in the creation of the content were:

- Imam ash-Shurunbulali's *Nur al-Idah* and its commentary, *Maraqi al-Falah*

- Imam al-Laqqani's *Jawharah at-Tawhid*

- Shaykh Salih Farfur's *ar-Risalah an-Nafi`ah fi `Ilm at-Tawhid*

- Imam Ibn Hisham's *as-Sirah an-Nabawiyyah* (including its English rendition by Martin Lings)

- Imam Ibn Kathir's *al-Bidayah wa an-Nihayah*

- and the many hadith collections compiled by the founder of Minhaj-ul-Quran, Shaykh-ul-Islam Dr Muhammad Tahir-ul-Qadri

The contents of these books have been adapted for children at an age appropriate level while keeping in consideration the specific needs and requirements of Western Muslims.

We are eager to hear from the wider community and to gain feedback regarding the series. For this purpose, we have set up an email address for you to send us your feedback. You can contact us at the following address: feedback@fmriuk.org.

Acknowledgements

Before closing, I would like to thank my co-editors, Jawed Iqbal Tahiri and Mariam Khalid, for their commitment and assistance in helping to prepare and develop the contents of this syllabus. I would also like to thank the Series Director, Tahseen Khalid, for his great determination and support in bringing this series to fruition.

I would also like to thank Bilal Hussain for his assistance in preparing the outline of the syllabus and the Textbook Review Team (Safina Nazir, Muhammad Zeeshan Qadri, Ali Akbar, Raffiq Patel and Dawood Mehmood) for their feedback and support. A special thank you goes to Ajmal Khan for the outstanding devotion he has shown in improving and further developing the design work.

I pray to Allah that He accepts our efforts and makes it a means of salvation for us in this life and the next, and we pray that this series becomes a means of uplifting the Ummah for generations to come.

Amin bi-jahi Sayyid al-Mursalin ﷺ

Waqas Ahmed Amin
Minhaj-ul-Quran Publications
1st Dhu al-Hijjah 1439 AH/12th August 2018 CE

Contents

My Din (Way of Life)
Lesson
1

Islam is our Din. A Din is a way of life. It teaches us how to live.

ISLAM

There are five pillars of Islam, which are important for every Muslim to perform. They are:

1 Shahadah

Saying and believing that there is no God but Allah and Prophet Muhammad ﷺ is the Messenger of Allah.

2 Salah

The five prayers that we pray every day.

3 Sawm

Fasting in the holy month of Ramadan.

4 Zakah

Giving charity to poor people.

5 Hajj

The journey to Makkah.

IMAN

Iman is our faith. It is the things that we believe in.
As Muslims, we believe in seven important things:

1

We believe in Allah, the One.

2

We believe in the angels.

3

We believe in the Holy Books.

4

We believe in the Prophets.

5

We believe in life after death.

6

We believe that all good and bad comes from Allah.

7

We believe in the Day of Judgement.

IHSAN

Ihsan is our relationship with Allah. It means that we remember Allah every day and know that He sees what we do all the time. Allah can see you, even if it is hidden. Allah can hear you when you whisper, and when you shout.

Our Din is everything that we do, everything we believe in and our relationship with Allah.

Cleanliness

Lesson 2

Cleanliness

Keeping clean is very important for Muslims. We should try to keep ourselves and everything around us clean.

How Can We Keep Clean?

Flush the toilet after you go to the bathroom.

Clean the toilet after using it and do not leave a mess behind.

Wash your hands with soap.

Have a shower or bath regularly.

Comb your hair and keep it tidy.

Trim your nails and do not let them grow too long.

Use a tissue to wipe your nose.

Brush your teeth twice a day; once in the morning when you wake up and once at night before going to bed.

Wash your hands before and after eating.

Wash your hands after touching anything dirty.

Do Wudu' before touching the Qur'an or praying.

Keep your clothes clean. Put your clothes and shoes away in wardrobes and drawers.

Keep your room tidy. Do not leave your books and toys lying around the house. Put them in their right place.

Keep your classroom clean and tidy.

Do not scribble on the walls or scratch the furniture.

Look after your mosque and school.

Do not throw rubbish on the floor. All rubbish should go in the bin.

Keeping Safe
Lesson
3

Prophet Muhammad ﷺ told us not to hurt ourselves or to hurt other people. As Muslims, we must look after ourselves and be careful.

Our parents and teachers know what is good for us. They care about us and look out for us. We must listen to our parents and teachers and do what they tell us. We should not hide anything from them, especially if it is something bad.

If you have done something wrong, you should tell your parent or teacher straightaway so that they can help you. If you do not, then something worse might happen.

The road can be a dangerous place. If you drop something, do not run after it straightaway. You should look around you first to see if it is safe and then go to get it.

Be careful when you cross the road. Hold the hand of an adult and do not run. Listen out for any cars that might be coming and look both ways before crossing the road. Use a crossing to cross over the road.

Be careful with things that are hot, especially the cooker or the iron. You should stay away from them because they can be hot and burn you.

Be careful with things that use electricity. Do not touch plug sockets and switches especially with wet hands.

Be careful with sharp things like scissors and knives. They can hurt you and put you in a lot of pain. Do not walk around with them because they can also hurt other people. Ask an adult to help you if you need to use them.

The Miracle of Commanding the Rain
Lesson
4

Once in Madinah, there was a time when there was no rain. This made life very hard for the people living in Madinah, because they had no water to drink.

During this time, Prophet Muhammad ﷺ was giving a talk to the people in his mosque.

A man stood up and said, "O Messenger of Allah! Our animals have died and our children are crying. So please pray to Allah to give us rain."

When the Prophet ﷺ heard this, he prayed to Allah for rain. The sky was clear, and nobody could see a single cloud in the sky, but as soon as the Prophet ﷺ raised his hands to pray, the sky was filled with clouds.

There were so many large clouds in the sky that they looked like mountains. When the people left the Prophet's mosque, they walked home in the pouring rain. It rained without stopping for a whole week!

The next week when the Prophet ﷺ was giving a talk to the people, the same man stood up and said, "O Messenger of Allah! Our things and our homes are getting damaged because of the rain, so please pray to Allah that He stops the pouring rain."

When the Prophet ﷺ heard this, he smiled. He raised his hands to pray and he said, "O Allah! Send the rain around us, but not on us."

As soon as the Prophet ﷺ prayed, the rain moved away from the city of Madinah where the people were, and it went to the area around the city. The sky in Madinah was clear and the sun was shining bright. It was still raining around the city of Madinah and the people there were happy with the well needed rain. (al-Bukhari)

Kalimah Tayyibah
Lesson 5

As Muslims, we say the Kalimah Tayyibah (Pure Word). The Kalimah Tayyibah tells us what we believe about Allah and Prophet Muhammad ﷺ. The Kalimah Tayyibah (Pure Word) is:

Laa ilaaha illallaahu Muhammadur Rasulullaah

There is no God but Allah; Muhammad ﷺ is the Messenger of Allah.

We believe in Allah:

- Allah is the name of the One True God.
- Allah is the One Who made everything.
- Allah is not a boy or a girl.
- Allah does not look like anybody.
- Allah has no children or family.

- Allah has no partner or helper.
- Allah sees and hears everything.
- Allah is the Greatest and the Most-Powerful.
- We say 'Subhaanahu wa ta`aalaa' after Allah's name.

We believe in Prophet Muhammad ﷺ:

- He is Allah's Prophet and Messenger.
- He is Allah's final Prophet and Messenger.
- He is the leader of all the Prophets.
- He is the best human being.
- He is Allah's most beloved creation.
- He is an example and guide for all Muslims.
- We say 'Sallallaahu `alayhi wa sallam' after his name.

Wudu' (Ablution)

Lesson

6

Wudu` is an important way to keep clean. We need to do Wudu` to pray and to touch the Qur'an.

When we do Wudu', we do the following things:

1

We wash both of our hands

2

We rinse our mouth

3
We rinse our nose

4
We wash our face

5
We wash both of our arms

6
We wipe our head with wet hands

7
We wipe our ears

8
We wash both of our feet

Good Manners

Lesson 7

It is very important for a Muslim to have good manners. A Muslim who has bad manners is not a good person.

Prophet Muhammad ﷺ had the best manners. He was sent by Allah to teach everyone good manners.

Having good manners means being nice to everybody. It means being kind and helpful to other people.

Some examples of good manners are:

Saying 'please'

Whenever we ask for something, we should say 'please'.

Saying 'thank you'

Whenever anyone gives us something or does something for us, we should say 'thank you'.

Saying 'excuse me'

Whenever we want to ask something from somebody, we should say 'excuse me' first.

Saying 'sorry'

If we accidentally do something wrong to somebody, or make a mistake, we should say 'sorry'.

Allah does not like people who are rude and behave badly. This is because rude people do not care about other people and how they make them feel.

Dos and Don'ts

Smile when you meet somebody.

Speak nicely and do not say 'what' in a rude way.

Do not take someone's thing without their permission.

Put things back in their right place.

Knock on the door before going in someone's room.

Do not be nosy and go into someone's room without their permission.

Do not disturb someone while they are asleep.

Do not make a lot of noise or shout.

Do not be grumpy and moody with other people.

Stand in the queue and do not push in.

Do not interrupt
someone while
they are speaking.

Do not throw
rubbish on
the floor. Put it
in the bin.

Do not put dirty
hands on walls
or furniture or
scribble on them.

Prophet Yunus عليه السلام

Lesson

8

The people of Ninevah used to worship idols. So, Allah decided to send Prophet Yunus عليه السلام to teach them that they should worship Allah only. But the people did not listen to him. They carried on worshipping idols and told Prophet Yunus عليه السلام that they will not listen to him.

After trying for a long time to make the people believe in Allah, he became worried for them because they would not listen to him. "The punishment of Allah will come to you in three days," warned Prophet Yunus عليه السلام. He then decided to leave that place.

When Prophet Yunus عليه السلام left, the people got worried about the punishment that was going to come for them, so they asked Allah for forgiveness. They also asked Allah to forgive them for treating Prophet Yunus عليه السلام badly. Allah forgave them and cancelled the punishment which was about to come to them.

When Prophet Yunus عليه السلام left Ninevah, he went on a ship. During the journey, the weather became very bad. The ship was in the middle of a huge storm. The ship was about to sink so the people tried to make the ship lighter by throwing things into the sea.

They had to throw one person into the sea to stop the ship from sinking. They decided to write down everyone's name, so it was fair and whoever's name was picked by chance, that person had to be thrown into the sea.

Prophet Yunus' name was chosen.

"Let's try again," said the people. They did not want to throw him into the sea because they knew that he was a good person. They tried again three times but each time his name was chosen.

Prophet Yunus ﷺ saw this as a sign from Allah and so he jumped off the ship. When he jumped, Allah sent a large whale to swallow him. Prophet Yunus ﷺ stayed in the belly of the whale.

After forty days, the whale dropped off Prophet Yunus ﷺ near the land. He went back home and saw that all of his people had asked Allah for forgiveness and had gone back to worshipping Allah, the One and Only God.

The Miracle of Creating Water

Lesson 9

One day, Prophet Muhammad ﷺ was travelling with his Companions. They were going to Makkah to perform the `Umrah.

When they came near Makkah, they rested in a place called Hudaybiyah. In those days there were no cars, so people travelled on camels and horses or they walked. It was a very hot day, and there was not a lot of water around.

They stayed in Hudaybiyah for a few days. They had drunk most of the water that they had with them and there was no water left to drink. There was only one small pot with a little bit of water in it.

Prophet Muhammad ﷺ took that pot of water and did Wudu' with it. Then he put his hand inside the pot.

When the Prophet ﷺ put his hand in the pot, the water started moving and bubbling inside the pot. It then started to come up slowly until it started flowing out from the sides of the pot like a running stream.

The Companions saw this amazing miracle.

"Look! The water is flowing from between the Prophet's fingers like fountains!" they cried in amazement.

With Allah's help, Prophet Muhammad ﷺ created water with his own hand. He told all his Companions to drink from the water and to fill their containers to keep for later.

The Companions were so happy to see this miracle. One by one they filled their containers with the water and they drank from it. They all would have died of thirst, but they were saved by the help of Allah.

One of the Companions called Jabir bin `Abdullah was there and he saw this miracle with his own eyes. A great scholar called Salim asked him how many people there were on that day. "There were 1500 of us on that day," Jabir replied, "but even if we were 100,000, the water would still have been enough for us all." (al-Bukhari)

Prophets
Lesson
10

Prophets were sent by Allah to guide people. As Muslims, we believe in the Prophets of Allah.

They are the best human beings and they do not disobey Allah.

Prophets are special people. They receive a special message from Allah and can talk to Him.

Prophets can do miracles. Allah gave special knowledge to them.

Prophets were sent to different parts of the world and to different people.

Prophets tell people to worship only Allah. They show people the right way.

As Muslims, we must:

- Believe in all the Prophets.
- Love the Prophets.
- Respect the Prophets.

The names of some of the greatest Prophets of Allah are:

1. **Prophet Adam** ﷺ - He was the first Prophet and the first man that Allah created.

2. **Prophet Nuh** ﷺ - The Prophet who built the Ark.

3. **Prophet Ibrahim** ﷺ - The Prophet who built the Ka`bah.

4. **Prophet Musa** ﷺ - The Prophet who was sent to fight against Pharaoh.

5. **Prophet `Isa** ﷺ - The Prophet who was raised up to Paradise and was saved by Allah.

6. **Prophet Muhammad** ﷺ - The last and final Prophet of Allah. The leader of all the Prophets and the one who Allah loves the most.

Peace and blessings be upon them all.

The Salah (Prayer)

Lesson 11

As Muslims, we pray to Allah only.
The Arabic word for prayer is Salah and it is one of
the five pillars of Islam.
We pray five times a day. The five daily prayers are:

Fajr

(The Dawn Prayer)

Zuhr

(The Afternoon Prayer)

`Asr

(The Late-Afternoon Prayer)

Maghrib

(The Evening Prayer)

`Isha'

(The Night Prayer)

Prophet Muhammad ﷺ taught us to pray in the following way:

1 Takbir at-Tahrimah

The Starting Position: Raise your hands up to your ears, with your palms facing out, thumbs touching your earlobes, and say the takbir (Allahu Akbar). Girls raise their hands to their shoulders only.

2 Qiyam

The Standing Position: Fold your arms, right hand on top of the left hand. Boys put their hands just under the belly button and keep their feet slightly apart. Girls put their hands on their chest and keep both their feet together.

3 Ruku`

The Bowing Position: Bow by bending forward until your back is flat like a table top. Put your hands on your knees. Girls keep their backs curved.

4 Qawmah

The Short Standing Position: Stand up from the Ruku' with your hands by your sides.

5 Sajdah

The First Prostration Position: Bow your head by putting your forehead and nose on the ground. Keep your hands placed on the ground next to your head.

6 Jalsah

The Short Sitting Position: Sit for a short time on your knees, with your back straight and your hands on your legs, facing down. Girls sit with their left side on the floor and feet flat towards the right side.

7 Sajdah

The Second Prostration Position: Bow your head by putting your forehead and nose on the ground. Keep your hands placed on the ground next to your head. Girls join their stomach to their thighs and place the arms and feet flat on the ground. Boys separate their stomach and thighs and keep their arms and feet raised upright from the floor.

8 Qa`dah

The Sitting Position: Same as 'Short Sitting Position'.

9 Salam

The Ending Position: End the prayer by turning your head towards the right shoulder and then the left shoulder.

Being Polite

Lesson 12

Allah loves people who are polite. Being polite means that you are nice to other people and that you do things in the right way. A Muslim should always be polite.

Polite people always smile when they meet somebody. They speak kindly to everybody and they do not behave badly with anyone.

Polite people do not shout at others or raise their voice to their elders. They listen to their elders like parents, grandparents and teachers and they always speak to them nicely.

Polite people do not snatch things from other people. They ask for permission first before using something and they wait patiently for their turn to use something.

Polite people do not argue with others. If someone is telling them something, they listen to them nicely and let them finish talking before saying anything.

Polite people are always on time. They do not be late. If they promise to do something, they keep their promise.

Polite people do not take too long doing something which will annoy someone else. They do things in their proper time.

Polite people meet their guests and visitors kindly. They ask them to come inside and to sit down. They bring food for them and ask them what they would like to drink. They spend time with their guests and do not ignore them.

Polite people eat respectfully. They do not spit out food or say that they do not like it. They sit down to eat, and they do not fill their plate with too much food. They take a little food at a time and they do not waste it.

The Story of `Uzayr عليه السلام

Lesson 13

One morning, `Uzayr عليه السلام left his farm and went on a trip. He rode his donkey and took some grapes and figs with him in a basket for his lunch.

As he was riding on his donkey, looking at the trees and the flowers, he came to a quiet and empty place. It was very hot and it looked broken down. There was nothing else there.

There was no sound; no buzzing bees or singing birds. There were no busy markets or streets and there was not even one other person there.

`Uzayr عليه السلام sat under a tree and ate some of his lunch. "I wonder what happened to this place?" he thought to himself.

He finished his lunch, stood up and said, "This place is so empty and broken down. How will Allah ever make this place busy and full of life again?"

`Uzayr عليه السلام was a friend of Allah so Allah wanted to show him how Powerful He is. So, as soon as `Uzayr عليه السلام said these words, Allah Almighty sent the Angel of Death to take his life and so `Uzayr عليه السلام died.

After one hundred years the same empty and broken-down place had changed. It was now very busy, and lots of people lived there.

Allah sent another Angel to `Uzayr ﷺ to bring him back to life. When `Uzayr ﷺ woke up the angel asked him, "How long do you think you have been asleep for?"

"Maybe a day, or part of a day?" `Uzayr ﷺ replied.

The Angel said, "`Uzayr, you were asleep for one hundred years!"

`Uzayr ﷺ was shocked and he looked around him and saw that the place was not empty and quiet anymore. It was busy and full of people. He also saw that the food he was eating was still fresh even after one hundred years, but his donkey had died and rotted away, only the bones were left on the ground.

When he saw all of this, `Uzayr ﷺ was amazed at the Power of Allah.

Allah brought `Uzayr's donkey back to life too. Then Allah said to `Uzayr ﷺ, "And look at your donkey, for We have made it a sign for the people. Look at the bones; how We bring them together and then cover them with skin."

When `Uzayr ﷺ saw this, he said, "Allah can do anything He wants."

Lesson 14

When Prophet Muhammad ﷺ moved to Madinah, the Prophet's mosque was built. It was a very simple mosque made of mud and bricks. There were no windows or doors. Tree trunks from date palm trees were used as pillars to hold the building up and the branches of the trees were used as a roof.

In this mosque, Prophet Muhammad ﷺ used to give talks to the people and while he did this, he would lean on the trunk of one of the date palm trees.

After a while, a pulpit was made by the Companions so that the Prophet ﷺ could sit down and give his talk. A pulpit is a special chair for the person who is giving a talk to the people.

When the Prophet ﷺ started to use the new pulpit, everyone heard the sound of crying. They were surprised and looked around to see where it was coming from. The sound was coming from the trunk of the date palm tree that the Prophet ﷺ used to lean on. The tree trunk was crying!

Prophet Muhammad ﷺ felt sorry for the tree trunk. He got off the pulpit and went to the tree trunk. He patted the tree trunk and put his arms around it. The tree trunk stopped crying in the same way that a baby stops crying when its mother picks it up.

If the Prophet ﷺ did not make the crying tree trunk feel better, it would not have stopped crying, and it would have still been crying today.

Prophet Muhammad ﷺ spoke to the tree and said, "I give you a choice of either becoming a young tree again or becoming a tree in Paradise." The tree trunk chose to be a tree in Paradise, so it was buried by the Companions in the mosque.

The tree loved the Prophet Muhammad ﷺ so much that it cried because it did not want to be away from him. If a tree loves the Prophet Muhammad ﷺ this much, then how much should we love the Prophet Muhammad ﷺ? (al-Bukhari)

Angels
Lesson 15

As Muslims,
we believe in angels.

Angels are a special creation of Allah.

Angels are Allah's servants.

Angels are made from light and they have wings.

Angels cannot do what they want. They do the jobs that Allah tells them to do.

They always listen to Allah and they never make mistakes.

Angels are not male or female.

Angels do not eat or drink.

Angels only like good and pure things.

Angels have different jobs to do. Some of the names of the great angels and their jobs are:

- **ANGEL JIBRA'IL:** Angel Jibra'il gives Allah's message and Holy Books to the Prophets. He is the leader of the angels.

- **ANGEL MIKA'IL:** Angel Mika'il controls the rain and the weather.

- **ANGEL `IZRA'IL:** Angel `Izra'il is the Angel of Death (Malak al-Mawt). He takes our soul at the time of death.

- **ANGEL ISRAFIL:** Angel Israfil will blow the trumpet on the Day of Judgement.

- There are two angels on the shoulders that stay with every person all the time. They write down all the things that we do. The angel on the right shoulder writes all the good things that we do. The angel on the left shoulder writes all the bad things that we do.

There are so many angels that we cannot count them. They are everywhere, and they bring blessings wherever they go.

The Islamic Calendar
Lesson 16

The Islamic calendar is called the 'Hijri' Calendar. It begins from the time that Prophet Muhammad ﷺ travelled from Makkah to Madinah.

The Islamic calendar is a lunar calendar. A lunar calendar is one that depends on the movements of the moon.

This means that a month in the Islamic calendar starts when the new crescent (hilal) of the moon can be seen. The lunar month is either 29 or 30 days.

There are twelve months
in the Hijri calendar and they are:

1.	Muharram	7.	Rajab
2.	Safar	8.	Sha`ban
3.	Rabi` al-Awwal	9.	Ramadan
4.	Rabi` ath-Thani	10.	Shawwal
5.	Jumada al-'Ula	11.	Dhu al-Qa`dah
6.	Jumada al-Ukhra	12.	Dhu al-Hijjah

These are some important
dates in the Islamic calendar:

10th Muharram:
Yawm `Ashura' and
the Battle of Karbala

12th Rabi` al-Awwal:
Mawlid an-Nabi (Birth
of Prophet Muhammad ﷺ)

27th Rajab:
Mi`raj an-Nabi ﷺ
(The Prophet's
Heavenly Journey)

15th Sha`ban:
Laylat al-Bara'ah
(The Night of Freedom)

27th Ramadan:
Laylat al-Qadr
(The Night of Power)

1st Shawwal:
Eid al-Fitr

9th Dhu al-Hijjah:
Yawm al-`Arafah

10th Dhu al-Hijjah:
Eid al-Adha

Being Kind and Helpful
Lesson 17

Be kind and helpful.
Allah loves those people who are kind and helpful to others. The kind and helpful person will be protected from the Hellfire and will be rewarded a lot by Allah.

Be kind and helpful to your parents. Help them around in the house and learn to do things by yourself. Listen to what they have to say and follow their instructions straightaway.

Be kind and helpful to your teacher. Be quiet when the teacher asks you to be quiet and listen when the teacher is talking.

Be kind and helpful to your elders. Always get up for them and give them your seat to sit on. If your elder is going to do something, always let them go first and wait for them patiently.

Be kind and helpful to your friends. Learn to play together nicely and share what you have with them. If one of them gets hurt, go to your teacher straightway and get some help.

Be kind and helpful to your neighbours. Do not make loud noises in the street or annoy them. Always smile when you see them and say kind words to them.

Be kind and helpful to animals. Do not hurt any animals or treat them badly. Give them water to drink and food to eat.

Be kind and helpful to everyone, whether they are Muslim or non-Muslim, older than you or younger than you.

Prophet Hud ﷺ
Lesson 18

Prophet Hud ﷺ was the great-great-grandson of Prophet Nuh ﷺ. He was sent to the people of `Ad. The people of `Ad were rich and powerful. Allah had made them the strongest people of that time, but they used to worship idols.

Prophet Hud ﷺ told his people that there is only One God, Allah. He tried to help them by saying, "You should worship the One God, Allah, and not the idols that you make with your own hands. You were made by Allah and you should be thankful to Him."

Over many years, he tried to make them listen. He kept on telling them about Allah's message, but they would not listen.

They said to Prophet Hud ﷺ, "Are you telling us that after we die and turn into dust, we will be brought back to life again?" "Yes. On the Day of Judgement, all of you will be asked about your actions in this life," Prophet Hud ﷺ replied. They laughed at him and made fun out of him.

Many years passed, and they still did not listen to the message given to them by Prophet Hud ﷺ. After many years of telling his people to worship Allah, Prophet Hud ﷺ warned his people of Allah's punishment.

"O people! Ask for forgiveness and change or else the punishment of Allah will destroy you all and none of you will survive," said Prophet Hud.

But the people did not care about what Prophet Hud ﷺ said to them. They just ignored his words and carried on disobeying Allah.

It had not rained for a very long time, so people did not have enough water to drink and there was not enough water for fruits and vegetables to grow.

One day, there were dark clouds in the sky. The people got happy seeing the clouds. "Look at the clouds! The rain will finally come to help us in this difficult time," said the people.

But Prophet Hud ﷺ warned them that this was the punishment of Allah. His people made fun out of him, not believing what he said.

As the dark clouds began to come nearer, they also brought a fast and fierce wind with them. There was a storm!

The storm was so strong that it ripped out trees from the ground and brought down all the tall buildings that were made by the people of `Ad. This wind was so powerful that it destroyed everything.

The next morning, when the wind stopped, nothing was left. All the people of `Ad were killed by this powerful storm and they were buried under the sand forever.

Lesson 19

When Prophet Muhammad ﷺ was forty years old, he got a special message from Allah. In this special message, Allah told him to tell others that he was His Prophet and Messenger.

The Prophet ﷺ told his beloved wife Khadijah, his best friend Abu Bakr and his cousin `Ali about this special message that Allah gave him, and they all believed in him and followed his message.

The Prophet ﷺ used to look after the poor and needy. He was kind to the orphans. The Prophet's wife Khadijah knew that her beloved husband was the Prophet of Allah because he was a truthful and honest man, who always looked after everyone. "I know you are the Prophet of Allah because you are always nice to everyone," she told him.

For three years, the Prophet ﷺ secretly told people about Islam. After this time, Allah told the Prophet ﷺ to openly tell everyone about Islam. So, the Prophet ﷺ climbed a mountain called Safa and called the people to come and hear what he had to say. People came to the mountain to hear the Prophet ﷺ because they knew what he had to say would be important.

"O Quraysh!" called the Prophet ﷺ. The people of Makkah gathered together at Mount Safa. "If I told you that there was an army in this valley ready to attack you, would you believe me?"

"Yes! We have never heard you say anything except the truth," they all replied.

Prophet Muhammad ﷺ told them, "Then listen to me. I have been sent by Allah to warn you and to tell you to worship only Him."

The people of Makkah knew the Prophet ﷺ from when he was born. They knew that he would not tell them a lie. This is why they listened to him and wanted to know what he was going to say.

Everyone knew that Prophet Muhammad ﷺ was really a Prophet. However, it was only those people who had good hearts who followed Islam and became Muslims straightaway. They knew Islam was a true religion because Prophet Muhammad ﷺ was a truthful man and he would not lie about anything important.

Holy Books

Lesson 20

As Muslims, we believe in the Holy Books. Allah sent Holy Books to help people. Allah gave the Holy Books to the Prophets, and the Prophets gave them to their people.

The Holy Books have Allah's special message in them. They tell us to worship Allah and not to make partners with Him. We must believe in the Holy Books.

We believe that Allah sent four Holy Books.

The Holy Books are:

1 The Tawrah which was given to Prophet Musa ﷺ.

2 The Zabur which was given to Prophet Dawud ﷺ.

3 The Injil which was given to Prophet `Isa ﷺ.

4 The Qur'an which was given to Prophet Muhammad ﷺ.

The Tawrah, Zabur and Injil are not with us anymore. These books have been changed and the original books that were given to the Prophets are lost. We believe in the books that were sent to the Prophets before they were changed.

The Qur'an is still with us today and it is the book we follow.

Some important things about the Qur'an are:

- The Qur'an is Allah's message given to Prophet Muhammad ﷺ.
- Angel Jibra'il used to bring this message from Allah and he gave it to Prophet Muhammad ﷺ little by little over 23 years.
- The Qur'an is the last Holy Book from Allah and there will be no Holy Book after it.
- The Qur'an has the original message that was written in the past Holy Books.
- The Qur'an is for all people and for all times.
- The Qur'an is a miracle of Prophet Muhammad ﷺ.

Fasting in Ramadan
Lesson 21

Fasting is when we do not eat or drink during the day. Muslims fast in the month of Ramadan, and it is one of the five pillars of Islam.

We have a meal before the fast called the 'Suhur'. This is an important meal which we have before the fast starts. At the end of the day, when the sun goes down and it begins to get dark, we break the fast and this meal is called 'Iftar'.

Fasting is a special kind of worship because no one can see that you are fasting. Allah loves people who fast because they fast only to make Him happy. `

We feel hungry by fasting and this helps us to know how the poor people feel. It teaches us to be kind and to think about other people.

During the month of Ramadan, we pray the Tarawih prayer in the night and we go to the mosque to pray this together. The Imam reads chapters from the Qur'an during this prayer and by the end of the month the whole Qur'an has been recited.

In the last ten nights of Ramadan, there is a special night called the 'Night of Power' (Laylat al-Qadr). This night is better than 1000 months. This night is very special because the Qur'an was sent down on this night.

Being Thankful

Lesson 22

Thank Allah for the bright sun and the beautiful moon. Thank Allah for having two eyes, a mouth and a nose. Thank Allah for your parents and family. Thank Allah for the yummy food that you eat. Thank Allah for everything.

Allah has given us so many blessings that we should be thankful to Him. If there is something that we do not have but would like to have, we should not be grumpy but instead ask Allah for it by making du`a.

We should think about the poor people in the world that do not have new clothes, a bed to sleep in or delicious food to eat. We know Allah is All-Powerful and can do what He wants. So let us make du`a and try to help the poor people.

We should be thankful to Allah that He blessed us with so many nice things. If we are thankful, Allah will give us more. We should not be ungrateful to Him.

We should also be thankful to other people as well. If someone does something good for us, we should thank them for it. The person who does not thank other people, he or she does not thank Allah.

Be thankful to your parents. They work hard to give you all the nice things that you have. They looked after you when you were small. If your parents say 'no' to you about something, you should listen to them and not start crying or keep asking.

Be thankful to your teachers, whether they are Muslims or not. They work hard to prepare for your lessons and to teach you. Listen to them and show them respect.

Prophet Salih عليه السلام

Lesson 23

Prophet Salih ﷺ was sent to the people of Thamud. The people of Thamud forgot about the worship of Allah and they started to worship idols. As they became richer and more powerful, they became more horrible to others.

Prophet Salih ﷺ reminded his people to worship only Allah and to stop worshipping false gods like idols. But, only a small number of the people listened to him and believed in him. Most of the people did not listen to his message.

Prophet Salih ﷺ carried on telling the people to worship the One God, Allah, but his people did not want to believe in him. They challenged him instead. "Show us a sign that you are truly the Prophet of Allah and are speaking the truth. Bring out a tall and beautiful she-camel from a rock," they said.

The people asked Prophet Salih ﷺ to do this very hard task because they believed that he could not do it. "If I show you this miracle, will you believe me and worship the One God, Allah?" Prophet Salih ﷺ asked them. "Yes, we will," they all replied.

So, Prophet Salih ﷺ prayed to Allah to show the people this miracle and the rock split apart and a tall, beautiful she-camel came walking out of the rock.

But seeing this great miracle, most of the people still did not want to believe. They turned away from it and carried on with their evil behaviour.

Everyone got their water from a water well. Prophet Salih ﷺ told the people to let the camel drink from the water well on one day and then they could drink from it the next day. The people did not like this idea and after some time they decided to kill the she-camel.

One day, while the camel was in the field, some young men came and killed the she-camel. Prophet Salih ﷺ was very sad when he found out about this.

Prophet Salih ﷺ told the people, "Ask for forgiveness from Allah. If you do not then you will get Allah's punishment." But they just laughed at him and did not care about what he said.

Prophet Salih ﷺ and his small group of followers left the people of Thamud and went somewhere else. After three days, while the people were sleeping in their homes, Allah sent a powerful earthquake and fierce winds. Their homes were destroyed and everyone living there died. They got the punishment that they did not believe in when Prophet Salih ﷺ tried to warn them.

Life After Death
Lesson 24

We were made by Allah to worship and obey Him, to make Him happy and to live as good people. This life is a test to see who is good and who is bad.

After death, Allah will bring us back to life again. We will be given a new life, and this is called 'life after death'.

There is a last day when this world will end. This last day is called the 'Day of Judgement'.

On this day, Allah will look at all our actions that we did in this life. If we are good, we will be rewarded for our good deeds. If we are bad, we will be punished for our bad deeds.

On the Day of Judgement, our actions will be measured on a big scale. All our good actions will be put on one side of the scale and all our bad actions will be put on the other side.

If our good actions are heavier than our bad actions, it means we were good in this life, so we will go to a special place called Paradise (Jannah). This is a beautiful place where good people will be rewarded by Allah.

If our bad actions are heavier than our good actions, it means we were bad in this life, so we will go to a horrible place called Hell (Jahannum). This is a very scary place where bad people will be punished by Allah.

Zakah and Sadaqah

Lesson 25

The Arabic word for charity is Sadaqah. Giving charity (Sadaqah) is a very important part of being a Muslim.

Sadaqah is one of the ways to help the poor people or anyone else who needs our help. Allah tells us to help the poor people and to look after them.

The homeless people, old people and orphans also need our help. We give Sadaqah to help them. It is a good way to make sure that everyone gets what they need so that no one is poor or hungry.

Sadaqah is not just about giving money to the poor people. It is about sharing and helping other people. We can even give charity by sharing our toys, clothes and sweets!

Sadaqah makes us think about other people and be generous to them. A person who gives a lot of charity is not greedy. The person who gives charity is a kind and caring person.

Giving charity is a way of thanking Allah. When we share with others, Allah gives us more.

We should do acts of charity every day by being kind and helpful to other people. Acts of charity can be smiling at someone, helping them with something or saying something kind to someone.

Muslims should give Sadaqah all the time. It can be given at any time, but once a year, adults have to give a small part of their saved money to the poor people. Giving this small amount of money every year is called Zakah, and it is one of the pillars of Islam.

Being Honest
Lesson 26

We should always tell the truth. Prophet Muhammad ﷺ always spoke the truth. He was known as 'as-Sadiq' (the truthful) and 'al-Amin' (the trustworthy).

Lying is a very big sin. Allah does not like people who lie. If you lie, it will get you into trouble, because after some time people will find out about it. If you lie a lot, then people will not trust you anymore, and they will not listen to you when you need their help.

Do not steal. Stealing is when you take something that is not yours. Ask for permission before taking anything that belongs to other people. If you want to buy something, make sure that you pay for it first before taking it. If you find something that has been left behind, do not take it.

Ask other people around you to see if it belongs to them. If the person who it belongs to asks for it, you should give it back to them. If no one says that it belongs to them, then tell your teacher or parent so they can keep it safe.

Be honest with everyone. Do not behave badly with someone just because they are different to you. Prophet Muhammad ﷺ was honest with everyone, even with people who treated him badly.

If someone asks you to look after their things, you should take care of them. Prophet Muhammad ﷺ used to look after other people's things, even if they were mean to him.

If someone tells you a secret, do not tell other people the secret. It is not nice telling someone's secret to other people. The only time you can tell a secret to an adult is when the person who told you the secret is getting hurt because of it like if they are being bullied or treated badly by someone.

When it is time for learning, you should stop playing and learn. If we play when it is learning time, then we are not being honest.

The Companions of the Cave

Lesson 27

About two hundred and fifty years after Prophet `Isa ﷺ, there lived an evil king. He worshipped idols and he did not like anyone who did not worship them. He made his people worship idols even if they did not want to.

From his people there were some young men who believed in Allah and did not worship idols. They were good men and they were nice to everybody and had good relations with the people and the king.

One day, the men decided to tell the king in front of all the people that they believed in Allah and did not worship idols. The king and the other people who worshipped idols did not like this.

"Catch them and lock them up!" ordered the king. The soldiers caught them, but the men escaped and ran away to the mountains. They saw a cave and they hid inside it. There were seven men and they had their dog with them.

The men felt tired, so they decided to rest and have a nap. They all fell asleep inside the cave, including the dog. Allah made them sleep for three hundred and nine years!

Allah looked after them while they were sleeping. To stop the cave from getting too hot Allah made the sun change direction every day so that the heat did not get inside. He also made the men turn from side to side after a while to stop their bodies from hurting.

At last, after three hundred and nine years they woke up.

"How long do you think we have been sleeping for?" they asked each other.

"Maybe a few hours," they all said.

They were hungry, so one of the men went to the shops to buy some food. When he tried to pay for the food with the money that he had, the shopkeepers saw that the coins he was trying to pay with were very old coins that were used many years ago.

After a while everybody realised that they were the young men who left three hundred years ago.

The men saw how the people had changed and they did not worship idols anymore. Everyone worshipped the One God, Allah. All the people wanted to meet these young men who left their homes so many years ago because they worshipped Allah.

But the young men did not want to be famous, so they prayed to Allah to take them somewhere else. "O Allah please take us away," they said.

When the young men died, they were buried in the cave. Some good people built a mosque at the mouth of the cave to get blessings, because these seven young men were Allah's friends who gave away everything that they had to make Allah happy.

Paradise and Hell

Lesson 28

Allah made Paradise (Jannah) and Hell (Jahannam). After Judgement Day, people will be sent to either Paradise (Jannah) or Hell (Jahannam).

Paradise (Jannah)

Good people will be sent to Paradise. They will live there forever. It is a reward for being good in this life.

In Paradise, Allah will give people anything that they wish for. Whenever they wish for something, they will get it straightaway.

Each person will be given a part of Paradise that will be bigger than the earth, as their home.

Paradise has lovely gardens with streams flowing in them, but they will not be like anything that we see on earth. Paradise will be so amazing that we cannot imagine it.

In Paradise, the people that did the most good actions will be in the company of the Prophets. They will also be able to see Allah the most.

Hell - Jahannam

Hell (Jahannam) is a horrible place. Those people who did not listen to Allah in this life and were cruel will be sent to Hell as a punishment.

Hell is a very big fire. Bad people will keep on burning in this fire. Shaytan will be in Hell too.

The people who believe in Allah but still did bad things will be sent to Hell and they will stay there for a long time. When Allah decides, He will take them out and send them to Paradise.

We should always pray that Allah protects us from the Hellfire and gives us a place in Paradise. Amin!

Lesson 29

The Hajj is a special journey a Muslim goes on to visit Makkah. It is one of the five pillars of Islam. As Muslims, we must perform Hajj at least once in our life, if we can.

A person who goes to Makkah to perform the Hajj is called a pilgrim. The pilgrim wears two white sheets called an Ihram.

Pilgrims walk around the Ka'bah seven times. This is called the Tawaf.

In the corner of the Ka`bah, there is a special stone from Paradise (Jannah). This stone is called al-Hajar al-Aswad (the Black Stone). The pilgrims kiss this stone.

There is a water-well underground next to the Ka'bah called Zamzam. The pilgrims drink its holy water.

There are two small mountains near the Ka`bah. They are called Safa and Marwah. The pilgrims run between these two mountains. This is called Sa`i.

The pilgrims also visit Madinah. Madinah is where Prophet Muhammad ﷺ is buried. Visiting Madinah before or after the Hajj is called Ziyarah.

The Prophet's mosque is in Madinah. It is called Masjid an-Nabawi. Inside the Prophet's mosque is the grave of Prophet Muhammad ﷺ. It is in a place called the Rawdah.

Next to the Prophet's grave is Riyad al-Jannah (the Garden of Paradise). This is where Prophet Muhammad ﷺ used to pray with his Companions.

We visit Madinah to give our Salam to Prophet Muhammad ﷺ and to pray in his mosque.

The Sirah Timeline

Lesson 30

0 (Birth)

Born in Makkah in the 'Year of the Elephants' on the 12th of Rabi` al-Awwal.

12 Years Old

Journey to Syria and meeting with Bahirah, the monk.

25 Years Old

The business trip to Syria and marriage to Lady Khadijah.

35 Years Old

Rebuilding of the Ka`bah and placing of the Black Stone in its corner.

40 Years Old

The first revelation in the cave of Hira'.

The beginning of the Prophetic mission. Telling people about Islam secretly.

43 Years Old

Telling people about Islam openly.

45 Years Old

Journey to Abyssinia.

47 Years Old

The boycott and the retreat to the mountain pass of Abu Talib.

50 Years Old

End of the boycott.
The Year of Sorrow
The Night Journey and the Heavenly Journey.

53 Years Old

The journey to Madinah
The building of Masjid an-Nabawi
(Prophet's Mosque)

54 Years Old

The Battle of Badr

55 Years Old

The Battle of Uhud

57 Years Old

The Battle of Khandaq (Trenches)

58 Years Old

The Treaty of Hudaybiyah

59 Years Old

The Conquest of Khaybar

60 Years Old

The Conquest of Makkah

62 Years Old

The Farewell Pilgrimage

63 Years Old

The Prophet ﷺ passes away

Lesson 31

We should look after our health.
It is a great blessing from Allah. We should
be thankful to Allah for our good health.

Allah made our bodies for us so that we could do good actions. We need to look after our bodies. If we look after our bodies, Allah will be pleased with us and reward us.

Stay away from bad eating habits. Do not eat too much or eat all the time. Prophet Muhammad ﷺ never used to fill his stomach when he ate food.

Stay away from unhealthy foods and snacks. Fizzy drinks, sweets and chocolates can damage your teeth. They have a lot of sugar which is not good for your health.

Eat less junk food and more fruits and vegetables. Wash the fruits and vegetables first before eating them. If you want, ask your parents to make them into drinks for you to enjoy.

Stay away from fast food and fried foods. This type of food is not good for you. When you get older it will make you unwell. Eat more homemade food cooked by your family because it is better for you.

You should be active and fit. Do not stay inside the house all day watching T.V. or playing computer games. Read a book, play in the garden or go to the park with your family.

Long hours on the computer and phone is not good for you. Take lots of breaks and do not sit down for too long. When you are watching screens, make sure that you sit away from the screen and keep the room well lit so that you do not harm your eyes.

Go out and get fresh air. Open the window and let fresh air come into your room. Have a picnic outside with your family or do a fun family activity together.

Lesson 32

As Muslims, we respect the Qur'an because every word in the Qur'an is from Allah.

We show respect to the Qur'an by putting it in a special place. We keep it wrapped up in a clean cover or cloth and we do not put our feet towards it. We should not put other books or anything else on top of the Qur'an.

We never put the Qur'an on the floor because this is disrespectful and very bad. We always keep the Qur'an higher than everything else.

We should only touch the Qur'an when we are clean and when we have Wudu'. Before opening or closing the Qur'an, we can kiss it out of respect if we want to.

When we read the Qur'an, we should wear clean clothes, sit in a clean place and cover our head. We should sit properly, and if we can, it is better to face the Qibla (the direction of the Ka`bah).

When we recite the Qur'an that we have learnt by heart, we can recite it while we are standing up or lying down.

We start reading the Qur'an by saying: A`udhu billaahi minash Shaytaanir rajeem; Bismillaahir Rahmaanir Raheem.

When we read the Qur'an, we should not talk to other people. If we want to talk about something, we should close the Qur'an first and then talk.

We should try to read the Qur'an in a beautiful voice. Do not rush when you are reading it. Read it properly with the rules of Tajwid. Not reading the Qur'an properly is a big sin.

If someone else is reading the Qur'an loudly, listen to it silently. Do not talk or make a noise.

NOTES